# Instant Pot®

# Cookbook: Collection of Best Step by Step Pressure Cooker Recipes.

MARIA SOBININA

BRILLIANTkitchenideas.com

# DEDICATION

This book is dedicated to my beautiful family and friends, as well as to you, my reader. I am happy to share the amazing joy of baking with you.

MARIA XOXO

# TABLE OF CONTENTS

# INSTANT POT® CILANTRO CHICKEN POT ROAST

## INGREDIENTS

3 Lbs. **Chicken**, raw, unfrozen

4 **Carrots**, medium, peeled

3 **Potatoes**, medium, peeled

1 cup **Broth**, vegetable, canned

2 cups **Onion**, chopped

3 cloves **Garlic**, diced

3 tablespoons **Cilantro**, fresh, chopped

1 tablespoon **Oil,** olive, extra-virgin

1 sprig **Rosemary**

¼ teaspoon **Salt,** pink, Himalayan

½ teaspoon **Pepper,** black, freshly ground

*Garnish:* Fresh parsley.

 *Equipment:*

*Instant Pot® , Knife Set, Food scale or measuring cups set.*

## PREPARATION

**Step 1:** Season chicken with salt and spices. Place rosemary in the cavity.

**Step 2:** Turn on the Instant Pot® . Choose the Sauté program with the Normal setting Add olive oil.

**Step 3.** Place chicken into the pot and sear on all sides for 3-4 minutes.

**Step 4:** After the chicken is seared, remove it and place vegetables into the pot: potatoes, carrots, and garlic. Cook for 3-4 minutes.

**Step 5:** Add vegetable broth and cilantro. Place chicken on top of the vegetables. Close the lid. Select the "Manual" program. Set the pressure on "High". If the Instant Pot® has a special poultry program, select the "Poultry" program.

**Step 6:** Set the timer for 25 minutes. After 25 minutes release the pressure.

Remove chicken and vegetables from the Instant Pot® . Slice chicken and garnish it with parsley.

Ready to serve.

*Store in the refrigerator for up to 5 days or in a freezer for up to one month.*

## INSTANT POT® CHUCK POT ROAST

## INGREDIENTS

3 Lbs. **Chuck roast**, raw, unfrozen

3 **Carrots**, medium, peeled, cubed

7 **Potatoes**, medium, peeled, cubed

1 cup **Broth**, beef, canned

¾ cup **Wine**, red

2 cups **Onion**, chopped

3 cloves **Garlic**, diced

3 tablespoons **Cilantro**, fresh, chopped

2 tablespoons **Flour**, all-purpose

1 tablespoon **Oil,** olive, extra-virgin

¼ teaspoon **Salt,** pink, Himalayan

½ teaspoon **Pepper,** black, freshly ground

*Equipment:*

*Instant Pot® , Knife Set, Food scale or measuring cups set.*

## PREPARATION

**Step 1:** Season chuck roast with salt and spices.

**Step 2:** Turn on the Instant Pot® . Choose the Sauté program with the Normal setting. Add olive oil.

**Step 3.** Place beef chuck into the pot and sear on all sides for 4-5 minutes.

**Step 4:** After the chuck roast is seared, remove it and place onion into the Instant Pot® and cook it for about 5 minutes occasionally stirring.

**Step 5:** Add garlic, spices, herbs and cook until all blends in. Add flour and cook for another two minutes periodically stirring. Add wine and stir again until all is incorporated and thickened.

**Step 6:** Add potatoes, carrots, cilantro, and beef broth. Place chuck roast on top of the vegetables.

**Step 7:** Set the timer for 60 minutes. After 60 minutes release the pressure.

Remove chuck roast and vegetables from Instant Pot® . Slice chuck roast and garnish it with parsley.

Ready to serve.

*Store in the refrigerator for up to 5 days or in a freezer for up to one month.*

## INSTANT POT® SALMON ROAST AND POTATOES

## INGREDIENTS

5 – 6 Oz **Salmon**, filets, unfrozen

3 **Carrots**, medium, peeled, cubed

16 **Potatoes**, small, peeled, halved

1 cup **Broth**, vegetable, canned

¾ cup **Wine**, white

3 cloves **Garlic**, diced

3 sprigs **Rosemary**

2 tablespoons **Flour**, all-purpose

1 tablespoon **Oil,** olive, extra-virgin

¼ teaspoon **Salt,** pink, Himalayan

½ teaspoon **Pepper,** black, freshly ground

*Equipment:*

*Instant Pot® , Knife Set, Food scale or measuring cups set.*

## PREPARATION

**Step 1:** Season salmon fillets with salt and spices.

**Step 2:** Turn on the Instant Pot® . Choose the Sauté program with the Normal setting Add olive oil.

**Step 3.** Place salmon fillets into the pot and sear on all sides for 2-3 minutes.

**Step 4:** After the salmon fillets are seared, remove them from the Instant Pot® . Place potatoes, carrots garlic, spices and herbs into the Instant Pot® . Add white wine and vegetable broth.

**Step 5:** Place steam racks on top of the vegetables. Place rosemary and salmon fillets on steam racks. Set the cooker to High Pressure for 5 minutes. After 5 minutes release the pressure.

**Step 6:** Remove the rack with salmon fillets from the Instant Pot® . Choose the Sauté program with the "Normal"setting. Add garlic and cook until softened. Add salt and pepper. Mash the potatoes until chunky.

Divide into portions. Ready to serve.

*Store in the refrigerator for up to 3 days or in a freezer for up to two weeks.*

# INSTANT POT® GARLIC BBQ BABY BACK RIBS

## INGREDIENTS

1 rack **Ribs,** baby-back, unfrozen

1 cup **BBQ Sauce**

1 cup **Broth,** beef, canned

¼ cup **Wine,** red, dry

3 cloves **Garlic,** diced

1 tablespoon **Oil,** olive, extra-virgin

¼ teaspoon **Salt,** pink, Himalayan

½ teaspoon **Pepper,** black, freshly ground

*Equipment:*

*Instant Pot® , Knife Set, Stem racks, Food scale or measuring cups set.*

## PREPARATION

**Step 1:** Season baby-back ribs with salt, garlic, and spices.

**Step 2:** Turn on the Instant Pot® . Add beef broth and wine into the pot. Place steam racks into the pot.

**Step 3.** Place ribs onto the racks. Set the cooker to High Pressure for 15 to 20 minutes. Release the pressure.

**Step 4:** Pre-heat oven to 425°F. Rub BBQ sauce into the ribs on all sides.

**Step 5:** Place the ribs onto the baking tray in the oven. Bake for 10 minutes. Broil for 2-3 minutes.

Ready to serve.

*Store in the refrigerator for up to 5 days or in a freezer for up to one month.*

## INSTANT POT® MUSHROOM BEEF STEW

## INGREDIENTS

3 Lbs. **Beef Stew**, raw, unfrozen

1 cup **Broth**, beef, canned

3 cups **Mushrooms,** white, chopped

2 cups **Onion**, chopped

3 cloves **Garlic**, diced

2 tablespoons **Flour**, all-purpose

2 tablespoons **Oil,** olive, extra-virgin

2 tablespoons **Soy**, sauce

¼ teaspoon **Salt,** pink, Himalayan

½ teaspoon **Pepper,** black, freshly ground

*Equipment:*

*Instant Pot® , Knife Set, Food scale or measuring cups set.*

## PREPARATION

**Step 1:** Season beef with salt and spices.

**Step 2:** Turn on the Instant Pot® . Choose the Sauté program with the Normal setting. Add olive oil.

**Step 3.** Place beef chuck into the pot and sear on all sides for 4-5 minutes.

**Step 4:** After the beef is seared, remove it and place onion into the Instant Pot® and cook it for about 5 minutes occasionally stirring.

**Step 5:** Add garlic, spices, herbs and cook until all blends in. Add flour and cook for another two minutes periodically stirring until all is incorporated and thickened.

**Step 6:** Place beef on top of the onions. Add soy sauce and beef broth.

**Step 7:** Set the timer for 40 minutes, then release the pressure. Add mudrooms, set to high pressure and cook for another 10 minutes. Release the pressure.

Ready to serve. You can serve it with noodles or potatoes.

*Store in the refrigerator for up to 5 days or in a freezer for up to one month.*

## Instant Pot® Chili

## INGREDIENTS

1 ½ Lbs. **Ground Beef**, raw, unfrozen

1 cup **Chicken Broth,** unsalted

1 cup **Onion**, chopped

3 cloves **Garlic**, finely diced

1 28 Oz can **Tomatoes**, crushed

2 19 Oz cans, **Red Kidney Beans**, drained, rinsed

2 tablespoons **Chili**, powder

1 tablespoon **Cumin**, seeds, ground

1 teaspoon **Oregano**, dried

2 tablespoons **Oil,** olive, extra-virgin

1 teaspoon **Salt,** pink, Himalayan

1 teaspoon **Sugar,** brown

1 teaspoon **Pepper,** black, freshly ground

2 tablespoons **Fish Sauce**

1 tablespoon **Soy Sauce**, light

3 tablespoons **Tomato**, paste

1 teaspoon **Cocoa Powder**, unsweetened

*Garnish:*

*Cheese, sour cream, lime, onion, cilantro.*

*Equipment:*

*Instant Pot® , Knife Set, Two small mixing bowls, Food scale or measuring cups set.*

## PREPARATION

**Step 1:** Season ground beef with salt and spices.

**Step 2:** Turn on the Instant Pot® . Choose the Sauté program with the Normal setting. Add olive oil.

**Step 3.** Place ground beef into the pot and cook for 4-5 minutes.

Ground beef will release juice after 5 minutes of cooking. Drain the juice into a small bowl. Set aside.

**Step 4:** Allow the remaining ground beef to cook stirring occasionally. After 5 to 7 minutes ground beef will become crispy and browned.

**Step 5:** In a small mixing bowl combine chicken broth, fish sauce, soy sauce, tomato paste, and cocoa powder.

**Step 6:** Add garlic, onion and cook until all blends in, for approximately 5 minutes.

**Step 7:** Pour chicken broth mixture, reserved ground beef juice, add kidney beans. Mix well and add crushed tomatoes on top. Cook for approximately 10 minutes on high pressure. Release the pressure.

Ready to serve. Garnish with your choice of garnish: cheese, sour cream, lime, onion, cilantro.

*Store in the refrigerator for up to 5 days or in a freezer for up to one month.*

## Instant Pot® Ginger Beef and Broccoli

**INGREDIENTS**

2 Lbs. **Steak**, chuck roast

1 cup **Chicken Broth,** unsalted

1 head **Broccoli**, separated on florets

4 cloves **Garlic**, diced

1 tablespoon **Ginger**, finely minced, fresh

1 tablespoon **Oil**, peanut, unrefined

1 teaspoon **Salt,** pink, Himalayan

1 teaspoon **Sugar,** brown

1 teaspoon **Pepper,** black, freshly ground

1 tablespoon **Soy Sauce**, light

1 tablespoon **Soy Sauce**, dark

1 teaspoon **Five Spice**, ground

¼ teaspoon **Sesame Oil**, unrefined

2 tablespoons **Cornstarch**

2 tablespoons **Water**, cold

## *Equipment:*

*Instant Pot® , Knife Set, Small mixing bowl, cutting board, Food scale or measuring cups set.*

## PREPARATION

**Step 1:** Season chuck steak with salt and black pepper.

**Step 2:** Turn on the Instant Pot® . Choose the Sauté program with the Normal setting. Add peanut oil.

**Step 3.** Place chuck stake into the Instant Pot® and sear on all sides for 5-7 minutes.

Remove the stake and place on a chopping board. Cut into 1-inch pieces.

**Step 4:** In a small mixing bowl combine chicken broth, light soy sauce, dark soy sauce, sesame oil, and five-spice powder. Pour the liquid into the Instant Pot® .

**Step 5:** Add chuck steak into the liquid. Let the mixture boil for 3-4 minutes.

**Step 6:** Turn off the pressure cooker. Place broccoli florets into the boiling liquid. Push "Keep Warm" button, close the lid and wait for 4 to 5 minutes.

Ready to serve. You can serve it with noodles or potatoes.

*Store in the refrigerator for up to 5 days or in a freezer for up to one month.*

## INSTANT POT® SPLIT PEA SOUP

## INGREDIENTS

2 Lbs. **Pork**, on a bone, smoked

1 Lbs. **Peas**, green, split

1 Lbs. **Carrots**, raw, chopped

5 cloves **Garlic**, diced

1 ½ cups **Onion**, chopped

5 cups **Chicken Broth,** unsalted

2 tablespoons **Oil**, olive, unrefined

1 teaspoon **Salt,** pink, Himalayan

1 teaspoon **Pepper,** black, freshly ground

½ teaspoon **Thyme**, dried

*Equipment:*

*Instant Pot® , Knife Set, Food scale or measuring cups set.*

## PREPARATION

**Step 1:** Turn on the Instant Pot® . Choose the Sauté program with the Normal setting. Add olive oil.

**Step 2.** Place chopped onion into the Instant Pot® . Add salt. Sauté for 2-3 minutes. Add garlic, thyme, chopped carrots, celery and sauté for another 2 minutes.

**Step 3:** Add chicken broth, green peas, and pork. Cook for 25 minutes. Release pressure.

Ready to serve.

*Store in the refrigerator for up to 5 days or in a freezer for up to one month.*

## INSTANT POT® POTATO SOUP

## INGREDIENTS

2 Lbs. **Potatoes**, gold, chopped

3 **Carrots**, raw, chopped

5 cloves **Garlic**, diced

1 ½ cups **Onion**, chopped

5 cups **Chicken Broth,** unsalted

1 cup **Heavy Cream** or **Coconut Cream**

2 tablespoons **Oil**, olive, unrefined

1 teaspoon **Salt,** pink, Himalayan

1 teaspoon **Pepper,** black, freshly ground

*Garnish:* chopped green onion, sour cream, freshly grated Parmesan cheese.

*Equipment:*

*Instant Pot® , Knife Set, Immersion blender, Paper towels, Food scale or measuring cups set.*

## PREPARATION

**Step 1:** Turn on the Instant Pot® . Choose the Sauté program with the Normal setting. Add bacon.

**Step 2:** Let bacon to crisp, constantly stirring it. Once it becomes crisp, set it aside on paper towels to drain fat.

**Step 3.** Place chopped onion into the Instant Pot® . Add salt. Sauté for 2-3 minutes. Add garlic, chopped carrots and sauté for another 2 minutes.

**Step 4:** Add chicken broth, potatoes and cook for 5 minutes plus fifteen minutes of Natural Release.

**Step 5:** Blend the soup with an immersion blender. Add heavy cream (or coconut cream) and blend the soup one more time.

Garnish with your choice of garnishes: chopped green onion, sour cream, freshly grated Parmesan cheese.

Ready to serve.

*Store in the refrigerator for up to 5 days or in a freezer for up to one month.*

## INSTANT POT® TOMATO SOUP

## INGREDIENTS

3 Lbs. **Tomatoes**, raw, quartered

1 Lbs. **Carrots**, raw, chopped

5 cloves **Garlic**, diced

1 cup **Onion**, white, chopped

4 cups **Chicken Broth,** unsalted

½ cup **Heavy Cream**

2 tablespoons **Olive Oil**, virgin, unrefined

2 ½ tablespoons **Rice**, jasmine

1 teaspoon **Basil**, dried

1 teaspoon **Salt,** pink, Himalayan

1 teaspoon **Pepper,** black, freshly ground

*Garnish:* Fresh basil.

*Equipment:*

*Instant Pot® , Knife Set, Immersion blender, Food scale or measuring cups set.*

# PREPARATION

**Step 1:** Preheat oven to 400°F. Place tomatoes into a baking tray. Sprinkle with olive oil, salt, and freshly ground black pepper. Roast for 45 - 60 minutes.

**Step 2:** Turn on the Instant Pot® . Choose the Sauté program with the Normal setting. Add olive oil.

**Step 3.** Place chopped onion into Instant Pot® . Add salt. Sauté for 2-3 minutes. Add garlic, chopped carrots and sauté for another 2 minutes.

**Step 4:** Add chicken broth.

**Step 5:** Add roasted tomatoes, dry jasmine rice, dried basil, thyme and cook for 3 minutes plus ten minutes of Natural Release.

**Step 6:** Blend the soup with an immersion blender. Add heavy cream and blend the soup one more time.

Garnish with fresh basil.

Ready to serve.

*Store in the refrigerator for up to 5 days or in a freezer for up to one month.*

# Instant Pot® Cauliflower Potato Soup

## INGREDIENTS

1 head **Cauliflower**, separated by florets

3 **Potatoes**, red, chopped

1 Lbs. **Carrots**, raw, chopped

5 cloves **Garlic**, diced

1 cup **Onion**, chopped

4 cups **Chicken Broth,** unsalted

6 slices **Bacon**, chopped

1 stalk **Onion**, green, chopped

½ cup **Heavy Cream**

1 teaspoon **Salt,** pink, Himalayan

1 teaspoon **Pepper,** black, freshly ground

*Garnish:* grated Parmesan cheese

*Equipment:*

*Instant Pot® , Knife Set, Immersion blender, Paper towels, Food scale or measuring cups set.*

# PREPARATION

**Step 1:** Preheat oven to 400°F. Place cauliflower into a baking tray. Sprinkle with olive oil, salt, and freshly ground black pepper. Roast for 45 - 60 minutes.

**Step 2:** Turn on the Instant Pot® . Choose the Sauté program with the Normal setting. Add bacon.

**Step 3:** Let bacon to crisp by constantly stirring it. Once it is crisp, set it aside on paper towels to drain fat.

**Step 4.** Place chopped onion into Instant Pot® . Add salt. Sauté for 2-3 minutes. Add garlic, chopped carrots, chopped potatoes and sauté for another 2 minutes.

**Step 5:** Add chicken broth.

**Step 6:** Add roasted cauliflower and cook for 3 minutes plus ten minutes of Natural Release.

**Step 7:** Blend the soup with an immersion blender. Add heavy cream and blend the soup one more time.

Garnish with Parmesan cheese.

Ready to serve.

*Store in the refrigerator for up to 5 days or in a freezer for up to one month.*

## Instant Pot® Sweet Potato Soup

## INGREDIENTS

3 Lbs. **Sweet Potatoes**, raw, quartered

1 Lbs. **Carrots**, raw, chopped

5 cloves **Garlic**, diced

1 cup **Onion**, chopped

4 cups **Chicken Broth,** unsalted

½ cup **Heavy Cream**

2 tablespoons **Oil**, olive, unrefined

¼ teaspoon **Cinnamon**, powder

1 teaspoon **Salt,** pink, Himalayan

1 teaspoon **Pepper,** black, freshly ground

*Equipment:*

*Instant Pot® , Knife Set, Immersion blender, Food scale or measuring cups set.*

## PREPARATION

**Step 1:** Preheat oven to 400°F. Place sweet potatoes into a baking tray. Sprinkle with olive oil, salt, and freshly ground black pepper. Roast for 45 - 60 minutes.

**Step 2:** Turn on the Instant Pot® . Choose the Sauté program with the Normal setting. Add olive oil.

**Step 3.** Place chopped onion into Instant Pot® . Add salt. Sauté for 2-3 minutes. Add garlic, chopped carrots and sauté for another 2 minutes.

**Step 4:** Add chicken broth.

**Step 5:** Add roasted sweet potatoes, cinnamon, and cook for 3 minutes plus ten minutes of Natural Release.

**Step 6:** Blend the soup with an immersion blender. Add heavy cream and blend the soup one more time.

Ready to serve.

*Store in the refrigerator for up to 5 days or in a freezer for up to one month.*

## Instant Pot® Lentils Soup

## INGREDIENTS

½ cup **Lentils**, green

½ cup **Lentils**, brown

3 **Carrots**, peeled, chopped

3 **Potatoes**, peeled, chopped

3 **Tomatoes**, fresh, chopped

1 **Onion**, white, shopped

1 **Pepper**, red, chopped

5 cloves **Garlic**, diced

1 cup **Onion**, chopped

4 cups **Chicken Broth,** unsalted

½ cup **Heavy Cream**

2 tablespoons **Oil**, olive, unrefined

1 teaspoon **Curry powder**, yellow

1 teaspoon **Cumin**, ground

1 teaspoon **Paprika**, ground

1 teaspoon **Salt,** pink, Himalayan

1 teaspoon **Pepper,** black, freshly ground

*Equipment:*

*Instant Pot® , Knife Set, Immersion blender, Food scale or measuring cups set.*

## PREPARATION

**Step 1:** Preheat oven to 400°F. Place carrots, tomatoes, potatoes, and peppers into a baking tray. Sprinkle with olive oil, salt, and freshly ground black pepper. Roast for 40 - 45 minutes.

**Step 2:** Turn on the Instant Pot® . Choose the Sauté program with the Normal setting. Add olive oil.

**Step 3.** Place chopped onion into the Instant Pot® . Add salt. Sauté for 2-3 minutes. Add garlic and sauté for another 1 minute.

**Step 4:** Add chicken broth.

**Step 5:** Add lentils, vegetables, cinnamon, and cook for five minutes plus fifteen minutes of Natural Release.

**Step 6:** Blend the soup with an immersion blender. Add heavy cream and blend the soup one more time.

Ready to serve.

*Store in the refrigerator for up to 5 days or in a freezer for up to one month.*

## INSTANT POT® CREAM OF CARROTS SOUP

**INGREDIENTS**

10 **Carrots**, fresh, chopped

2 **Potatoes**, peeled, chopped

1 **Onion**, white, finely shopped

1 **Pepper**, red, chopped

3 cloves **Garlic**, diced

1 cup **Onion**, chopped

5 cups **Chicken Broth,** unsalted

½ cup **Heavy Cream** or **Coconut Cream**

2 tablespoons **Oil**, olive, unrefined

1 teaspoon **Cumin**, ground

1 teaspoon **Paprika**, ground

1 teaspoon **Salt,** pink, Himalayan

1 teaspoon **Pepper,** black, freshly ground

*Equipment:*

*Instant Pot® , Knife Set, Immersion blender, Food scale or measuring cups set.*

## PREPARATION

**Step 1:** Preheat oven to 400°F. Place carrots, potatoes, and pepper into a baking tray. Sprinkle with olive oil, salt, and freshly ground black pepper. Roast for 45 minutes.

**Step 2:** Turn on the Instant Pot® . Choose the Sauté program with the Normal setting. Add olive oil.

**Step 3.** Place chopped onion into the Instant Pot® . Add salt. Sauté for 2-3 minutes. Add garlic and sauté for another 1 minute.

**Step 4:** Add chicken broth.

**Step 5:** Add roasted vegetables, spices, salt and cook for three minutes plus ten minutes of Natural Release.

**Step 6:** Blend the soup with an immersion blender. Add heavy cream and blend the soup one more time.

Ready to serve.

*Store in the refrigerator for up to 5 days or in a freezer for up to one month.*

## INSTANT POT® CREAM OF PUMPKIN

**INGREDIENTS**

1 **Pumpkin**, medium size, fresh, chopped

1 **Onion**, white, finely shopped

1 **Pepper**, red, chopped

5 cloves **Garlic**, diced

1 cup **Onion**, chopped

5 cups **Chicken Broth,** unsalted

½ cup **Heavy Cream**

½ cup **Coconut cream**

2 tablespoons **Oil**, olive, unrefined

1 teaspoon **Cinnamon**, ground

1 teaspoon **Paprika**, ground

1 teaspoon **Salt,** pink, Himalayan

1 teaspoon **Pepper,** black, freshly ground

*Equipment:*

*Instant Pot® , Knife Set, Immersion blender, Food scale or measuring cups set.*

## PREPARATION

**Step 1:** Preheat oven to 400°F. Place pumpkin and pepper into a baking tray. Sprinkle with olive oil, salt, and freshly ground black pepper. Roast for 45-55 minutes.

**Step 2:** Turn on the Instant Pot® . Choose the Sauté program with the Normal setting. Add olive oil.

**Step 3.** Place chopped onion into the Instant Pot® . Add salt. Sauté for 2-3 minutes. Add garlic and sauté for another 1 minute.

**Step 4:** Add chicken broth.

**Step 5:** Add roasted vegetables, spices, salt and cook for 3 minutes plus 10 minutes of Natural Release.

**Step 6:** Blend the soup with an immersion blender. Add heavy cream, coconut cream and blend the soup one more time.

Ready to serve.

*Store in the refrigerator for up to 5 days or in a freezer for up to one month.*

## INSTANT POT® CREAMY BABY POTATOES

## INGREDIENTS

2 Lbs. **Baby Potatoes**

1 cup **Water**, cold

1 teaspoon **Salt,** pink, Himalayan

1 teaspoon **Pepper,** black, freshly ground

*Garnish:* Dill, sour cream, minced garlic.

*Equipment:*

*Instant Pot® , Knife Set, Stainless steel steaming basket, Immersion blender (optional), Food scale or measuring cups set.*

## PREPARATION

**Step 1:** Turn on the Instant Pot® . Add cold water, salt, and pepper, and place a stainless steel steamer basket into the Instant Pot® . Place potatoes into the steaming basket. Cook at high pressure for 12-15 minutes. Quick Release.

Garnish with sour cream, minced garlic, and dill. *Optional:* mash with an immersion blender for mashed potatoes.

Ready to serve.

*Store in the refrigerator for up to 5 days or in a freezer for up to one month.*

## INSTANT POT® ROASTED BABY POTATOES

## INGREDIENTS

2 Lbs. **Baby Potatoes**

1 cup **Water**, cold

2 tablespoons **Oil**, olive, unrefined

4 cloves **Garlic**, minced

1 teaspoon **Salt,** pink, Himalayan

1 teaspoon **Pepper,** black, freshly ground

*Garnish:* Dill, Sour cream.

*Equipment:*

*Instant Pot® , Knife Set, Stainless steel steamer basket, Food scale or measuring cups set.*

## PREPARATION

**Step 1:** Turn on the Instant Pot® . Add cold water, salt, and pepper, and place a stainless steel steamer basket into the Instant Pot® . Place potatoes into the steaming basket. Cook at high pressure for 10-12 minutes. Quick release. Turn off the Instant Pot® .

**Step 2:** Drain the water and towel dry the Instant Pot® .

**Step 3:** Turn on the Instant Pot® . Choose the Sauté program with the Normal setting. Add olive oil when Instant Pot® heats up.

**Step 4:** Add steamed potatoes, spices, garlic, salt and let the potatoes to brown.

Garnish with sour cream and dill.

Ready to serve.

*Store in the refrigerator for up to 5 days or in a freezer for up to one month.*

## INSTANT POT® PINEAPPLE HAM
## INGREDIENTS

1 9 Lbs. **Ham**, bone-in, thick

I can **Pineapple**, crushed

¼ cup **Honey**, raw

¼ cup **Sugar**, brown

2 tablespoons **Cornstarch**

3 tablespoons **Water**, cold, tap

2 tablespoons, **Mustard**, Dijon

*Equipment:*

*Instant Pot® , Knife Set, Small mixing bowl, Cutting board, Food scale or measuring cups set.*

## PREPARATION

**Step 1:** Turn on the Instant Pot® . Add Dijon mustard and crushed pineapples. Glaze ham with honey, place ham on top. Cook at a high pressure for 20 minutes plus 30 minutes Natural Release (for 8 to 9 Lbs. ham).

**Step 2:** Remove ham from the pressure cooker and place onto a cutting board. Turn off the pressure cooker.

**Step 3**: Prepare pineapple sauce. Turn the pressure cooker on. Choose the Sauté program with the Normal setting. Bring the sauce to simmering. Add brown sugar and cook for another minute.

**Step 4:** In a small mixing bowl mix cornstarch with cold water. Slowly add cornstarch mixture to pineapple sauce.

Cut the ham and serve with the pineapple sauce.

*Store in the refrigerator for up to 5 days or in a freezer for up to one month.*

## INSTANT POT® CHOCOLATE PARADISE LAVA CAKE

## INGREDIENTS

6 Oz **Chocolate**, dark, 80% cocoa

3 **Eggs**, large, pasteurized

3 **Egg yolks**, pasteurized

1 cup **Butter**, unsalted

2 tablespoon **Flour**, all-purpose

½ cup **Sugar**, white, granulated

1 teaspoon **Cognac** (optional)

½ teaspoon **Vanilla**, pure extract

1 cup **Water**, cold

*Equipment:*

*Instant Pot® , Spatula, Hand or stand mixer, Knife Set, Small heat-proof pot, Large mixing bowl, 4 6 Oz ramekins, Stainless steel trivet, Food scale or measuring cups set.*

## PREPARATION

**Step 1:** Over the stove in a small pot melt dark chocolate and butter.

**Step 2:** In a large mixing bowl combine eggs, egg yolks, and sugar. Beat on medium speed with a hand or stand mixer for 1-2 minutes.

**Step 3:** Slowly pour chocolate mixture into egg mixture. Add flour, Cognac (optional), and vanilla. Mix with a spatula to incorporate.

**Step 4:** Pour chocolate cake mixture evenly into 4 ramekins.

**Step 5:** Place a stainless steel trivet inside the Instant Pot®. Pour one cup of water inside of the Instant Pot®. Place ramekins with chocolate batter onto the trivet. Pressure cook for 7-10 minutes with a Quick Release.

Remove ramekins from the Instant Pot®. Set aside on a countertop to cool. Ready to serve once cooled.

*Store in the refrigerator for up to 5 days or in a freezer for up to one month.*

## INSTANT POT® MAPLE-CANDIED PECANS

## INGREDIENTS

3 cups **Pecans**, halved

½ cup **Maple Syrup**

3 tablespoons **Butter**, unsalted

¼ teaspoon **Cinnamon,** ground

¼ teaspoon **Salt,** pink, Himalayan

*Equipment:*

*Instant Pot® , Knife Set, Food scale or measuring cups set.*

## PREPARATION

**Step 1:** Turn on the Instant Pot® . Choose the Sauté program with the Normal setting. Add butter. Heat up for 1-2 minutes.

**Step 2:** Add maple syrup into the Instant Pot® . Once the syrup is slightly bubbling, add pecans and pink salt. Stir to cover pecans evenly. Let them heat up for 3-4 minutes constantly stirring.

**Step 3:** Place maple-coated pecans in a single layer on to the parchment paper. Let them dry.

Ready to serve.

*Store in the refrigerator for up to 30 days or in a freezer for up to three months.*

## INSTANT POT® RICOTTA LASAGNA

## INGREDIENTS

9 **Lasagna noodles**, oven ready

1 Lbs. **Ground beef,** 85 %

1 **Onion**, chopped

1 cup **Water**, cold

3 **Garlic** cloves, minced

2 cups **Mozzarella cheese**, shredded

½ cup **Parmesan cheese**, shredded

1 ½ cups **Ricotta cheese**

1 **Egg**, large

¼ teaspoon **Salt,** pink, Himalayan

½ teaspoon **Pepper,** black, freshly ground

1 teaspoon **Oregano**, dried

*Equipment:*

*Instant Pot® , Knife Set, Small mixing bowl, 7-inch Springform pan, Parchment paper, Food scale or measuring cups set.*

# PREPARATION

**Step 1:** Season ground beef with salt and spices.

**Step 2:** Turn on the Instant Pot® . Choose the Sauté program with the Normal setting. Add olive oil.

**Step 3.** Place ground beef into the pot and sear on all sides for 4-5 minutes.

**Step 4:** After the beef is seared, remove it and place onion into the Instant Pot® and cook it for about 5 minutes occasionally stirring.

**Step 5:** Add garlic, spices, herbs and cook until all blends in. Add ground beef back and stir until all is incorporated. Remove from Instant Pot® and place into a small mixing bowl. Turn off the Instant Pot® .

**Step 6:** In a mixing bowl, beat one large egg, add Ricotta cheese. Season with oregano, ground black pepper, and salt. Mix well with a spatula and set aside.

**Step 7:** Assemble lasagna. Line springform pan with parchment paper. Place the first layer of lasagna noodles on top of the parchment paper. (Break them as needed to fit into the springform).

Place ¼ of the ground beef mixture on top of the noodles. Then place ¼ of the ricotta cheese mixture on top of ground beef. Spread evenly. Add shredded mozzarella cheese on top.

Repeat for all other layers.

**Step 8:** Pour cold water into the Instant Pot® , then place a trivet. Place springform pan onto the trivet. Close lid, then pressure cook at High Pressure for 25 minutes plus ten minutes of Natural Release.

Ready to serve.

*Store in the refrigerator for up to 5 days or in a freezer for up to one month.*

*Email us at: At Maria@BrilliantKitchenIdeas.com*

**MARIA SOBININA**
**BRILLIANT kitchen ideas**

Would you like to learn cooking
techniques and tips?

Visit us at BRILLIANTkitchenideas.com

We have series of educational videos on
cooking.

**www. BRILLIANTkitchenideas.com**

Printed in Great Britain
by Amazon